I0022083

Table of Contents

How to Make Your Programs Run Hundreds to Thousands Times Faster Without Giving up Reliability and Ease of Programming 2

  Introduction 2

  Frequently Asked Questions 3

  Static vs dynamic typing 6

    Introduction 6

    Dynamic typing explained 8

What would be my choice of programming language if I was ordered to write a nuclear weapon control system? 10

Which compiler should I use? 19

  Comparison 20

  Package and/or binary availability, by platform and compiler 24

  Experimental compilers and forks 27

How to Make Your Programs Run Hundreds to Thousands Times Faster Without Giving up Reliability and Ease of Programming

Introduction

D programming language is the newest and the **only** technology that is both:

- high performance
- rapid development
- reliable

High performance means that your software is expected to load at least about 10 times faster (for SSD disks) and run **hundreds to thousands**

of times faster than most modern software and also use much less memory and produce less heat at the CPU.

Rapid development means that you do the project quickly. D programming is as easy for experienced programmers as Python or Ruby programming, if not easier thanks to higher reliability (see below) and thus less time to debug.

Reliable means that you use no less (maybe more) reliable technologies than in the atomic powerplant that powers your house and nuclear rockets and airplanes, not what other developers do.

Frequently Asked Questions

How can it be thousands of times faster?

1. D compiler produces directly CPU machine code, not an intermediary code.

2. D programming language is a statically typed language (see below).

These two features together allow programs to run hundreds to thousands of times faster.

Which reliability features D has?

- strict identifiers
- static types
- both dynamic and static asserts
- type traits checking
- automatic memory deallocation
- no pointer arithmetic when unnecessary
- array range checking
- complex program logic checking at compile time

What are the advantages of D?

- advanced programming language (not less than to say Python or Ruby) allowing to easily solve almost all kinds of programming problems

- very high speed (on par with C, C++, Ada, Rust)
- reliable (not worse than Ada, comparable with Rust)
- the reasoning at compile time

Is D the very best programming language?

Yes as of 2019. (Well, some people would argue that Rust is better.) Well, almost, D isn't the best tool for proving the correctness of math theorems, in **all** other applications which I know D is the best one.

Is D open source?

Yes.

What are the debug and release modes?

In D there are basically two modes of created software: debug and release. Debug mode may be a few times slower, but release mode software may crash randomly in the case of errors rather than shut down the program more correctly. It is your choice, what you need more: reliability or speed.

Static vs dynamic typing

Introduction

Programming languages are of two categories:

1. *statically* (or what is the same *strongly*) typed
2. *dynamically* typed

The distinction is that in a dynamically typed language a variable can hold any object (and moreover the type of the variable can change while programs run), while in a statically typed language a variable can hold only an object of a certain type.

At first, it seems that dynamic typing makes programming easier, but it comes at a high cost:

1. Programs in dynamic languages work **much** slower and use more memory. Moreover is too hard to write an

optimizing compiler for a dynamic language, so programs work even slower.

2. Dynamic languages don't check value types what makes it *very* easy to make an error. Probably more than 50% of all programming errors are a wrong variable type in a dynamic language. Beware of unreliability.

In the past most languages used were static. It is understandable: Computers were slow and they needed fast languages.

In recent years dynamic languages gained popularity because they make programming easier.

But recently there was an unnoticed revolution: It was created D programming language, a static language which is as powerful (if not more) as dynamic languages. Now nothing prevents you to have both: high speed and reliability as well as a language with powerful features easy to use, to write short, understandable programs.

Dynamic languages now should mostly go to history. D is better.

Dynamic typing explained

Static typing is mostly simple: After compilation, a variable is either a word (such as a 64-bit integer) in computer memory or a group of nearby words or a set of such interrelated objects.

To make it even faster, variables can often be stored directly in a CPU register rather than in RAM.

Dynamic typing is more complex to implement (and it is, therefore, slower): A variable consists of:

- a memory word specifying its type (remember, in a dynamic language a variable can have multiple types and even change its type)
- a pointer to a memory location where the variable is placed

- a word or sequence of words holding the actual value

You see, it takes more memory. But the main problem is that memory for the variable value needs to be allocated/deallocated (and it is a slow operation) while the variable is created, changed, or destroyed. Almost every operation requires memory allocation. Also, as I said above the complexity of doing this prevents optimizing the program to make it fast. For example, we cannot store a dynamic variable in a CPU register. This is the reasons why dynamic is sometimes hundreds or thousands of times slower.

What would be my choice of programming language if I was ordered to write a nuclear weapon control system?

What would be my choice of programming language if I was ordered to write a nuclear weapon control system, control of a nuclear plant, flight control system, or some other software which life of many people depends on? The following choice would be considered:

- assembler
- C
- C++
- Ada

- Go

- D

- Python

- Ruby

- Rust

- Haskell

- a variant of ML such as OcamML

- a mathematical proof assistant such as LEAN, Coq, Isabelle (definitely not Mizar as it has bad documentation)

Assembler, while technically being the most reliable variant, is bad for our task, as it is to complex (and so unreliable) to write software in it.

Language	Ada	D	C	Python	Ruby	Coq	Lean
Compiler quali	low	high	high	high	high	probably very	probably very

ty						good	good, despite of written in C++
Power of expression	good	very good	low	very good	very good	almost the most powerful programming language in the world	the most powerful programming language in the world
Simplicity of syntax and semantics	mediocre	mediocre	good	very good	very good	very hard	probably very good
Ease of prog	mediocre	mediocre	bad	very good	very good	extremely hard	extremely hard

ram ming							
General syntax and semantic reliability	high, but not perfect	high, but not perfect	very low	syntax reliable, semantics not quite	syntax reliable, semantics not quite	not very reliable syntax, but compensated by extremely powerful semantic checking	not very reliable syntax, but compensated by extremely powerful semantic checking
Protection against typos in IDs	yes	yes	yes	no	no	yes	yes
Strong	yes	yes	yes	no	no	when wante	when wante

typing						d	d
Exceptions	yes, but without subclassing	yes	not quite	yes	yes	yes	yes
Subtyping	yes	no	no	no	no	yes	yes
Out-of-range checking	yes (turnable off)	no, but can be done with a library	no	no need as integers are unbounded	no need as integers are unbounded	yes	yes
Modularity and encapsulation	yes	yes	no	yes, but without enforced private	yes, but without enforced private	yes	yes

				mem bers	mem bers		
Fixed point types	yes	no, but can be done with a librar y	no	when wante d	when wante d	essen tially, yes	essent ially, yes
Side effect s	partly unreli able	partly unreli able	unreli able	yes	yes	no	no
asser t, pre, post, and class invar iants	yes	yes	only assert	assert only	assert only	essen tially, yes	essent ially, yes
static asser t and chec king by	no	yes	no	no	no	yes	yes

16

traits							
Dangling references, errors in memory deallocation	unreliable	no, except of low-level programming	unreliable	usually no	usually no	no	no
Multi-tasking	yes	yes	can be done	yes, but no multicore support on the default interpreter	yes, but no multicore support on the default interpreter	no(?)	no(?)
Deliberate unsaf	yes	yes	yes	almost no	almost no	axioms	axioms

e features							
Formal checking	partially, with Spark	no	no	no	no	yes	yes
Speed	very high	very high	very high	very low	very low	extremely slow	extremely slow
Bug fixing	in practice, only for paid customers (what negatively affects all customers including paid	taken seriously	taken seriously	taken seriously	taken seriously	taken seriously	taken seriously

	ones)						

All considered languages have more or less powerful debuggers. There are some bugs in the debuggers but I am not enough expert in this topic.

Ada is finally dead, finally killed by Rust and D as competitors better in practice.

Main Ada reliability features: exceptions, private entities, subtypes and derived types, ranged integer types, discriminants, invariants and assertions. D has some but not all of these features (particularly no subtypes in D, but will explain that neverteless D is more reliable than Ada).

Ada was designed to be reliable, but in practice it is very unreliable: There is no good Ada compiler! GNAT (the Ada part of GCC) has far too many bugs as my unfortunate experience with Ada showed. Expect a thermonuclear war at any second, it is assumed that rockets control systems are made with Ada, probably this buggy GNAT (aren't others even less reliable?) The same may concern nuclear plants control.

So my choice would be either Rust, D, Haskell, or a variant of ML. I also would consider Lean or Coq provided I could be able to hire enough high qualified experts (but for a system of intercepting rockets this would not work, as we need speed). Well, I don't know Rust, Haskell, and ML well, but this article is written for real nuclear engineers and anyone who needs very high reliability not for myself.

So if to make a nuclear weapon control system, I would choose either Rust or D.

Which compiler should I use?

(This chapter is licensed under CC-BY-SA 3.0.)

For beginners, DMD is the recommended choice, as it is the implementation closest to the D Language Specification. Otherwise, the best choice depends on the project's needs, the target platforms, and personal preferences. GDC and LDC both generate substantially faster binaries than DMD.

Comparison

	DMD	**GDC**	**LDC**
Platforms	Windows Linux OS X FreeBSD	Windows (alpha) Linux OS X (untested) FreeBSD	Windows Linux OS X FreeBSD OpenSolaris iOS

		(untested)	(alpha) Android
Architectures	i386 amd64	Complete (runtime / standard library) support: i386 amd64 x32 armel armhf Partial or bare-metal only support (packages for gdc in debian): alpha arm64 (aarch64)	Complete (runtime / standard library) support: i386 amd64 armel armhf Near-complete support: arm64 (aarch64) ppc ppc64 ppc64el mips64 Partial or

		hppa hurd-i386 kfreebsd-amd64 kfreebsd-i386 m68k mips mipsel ppc pcc64 ppc64el s390x sparc64	bare-metal only support: mips s390x
Distrib ution	Source Multi-platform source/binary archive Multi-platform installer (<u>DVM</u>) Windows installer OS X package	Source Windows / Linux binary archive Debian/Ubuntu repository Gentoo repository	Source Windows / Linux / OS X binary archive Debian/U buntu repository Fedora

		Archlinux repository	repository Gentoo repository FreeBSD repository GNU Guix Nix/NixOS package (for NixOS, other Linux and OS X)
	(.dmg) Debian/Ubuntu package (.deb) Fedora package (.rpm) OpenSUSE (.rpm) package Debian/Ubuntu repository via http://d-apt.sourceforge.net OS-X homebrew and macports repositories Nix/NixOS package (for NixOS, other Linux and OS X)		
Backend	DMD (DMC fork)	GCC	LLVM
License	Boost	GPL 3 or	LDC-

		later	specific code: 3-clause BSD
Inline assembler	DMD Intel-like syntax (i386/amd64)	GCC syntax (all targets)	DMD Intel-like syntax (i386/amd64) GCC syntax (all targets) LLVM inline IR
SIMD	Partial (?)	Partial (?)	Partial (?)
Phobos as a shared library	Linux FreeBSD ?		Linux
Building D code as shared library	Linux FreeBSD ? Windows ?		Linux OS X

Dynamic loading of D shared libraries	Linux		Linux OS X
Linux specific			
Object file format	ELF	ELF	ELF
Mac specific			
Object file format	Mach-O	Mach-O	Mach-O
Windows specific			
Object file format	OMF (32) / COFF (32 & 64)	COFF	COFF

Package and/or binary availability, by platform and compiler

Some unofficial repositories and downloads are listed here, but of course many more do exist. With a little searching, you may be able to find something more up to date for your chosen OS.

Very old compilers are (mostly) omitted, as they are unlikely to be of interest to users.

Platform	Compiler		
	DMD	GDC	LDC
Windows	Manual download Chocolatey	Manual download	Manual download
OS X	Homebrew MacPorts Nix Manual		Homebrew Nix Manual download

	download		
iOS			Manual download
Android			Manual download Instructions on setup, including a native package
Linux (generic)	Manual download	Manual download	Manual download Source (ARM/Linux cross-compiler)
Cross-platform	DVM (Any version)		
Distribution-specific packages			
Debian	Manual	stable	stable

	download APT repository	testing unstable	testing unstable
Ubuntu	Manual download APT repository	gdc	ldc
Fedora	Manual download		See https://apps.fedoraproject.org/packages/ldc
OpenSuse	devel:languages:D		devel:languages:D home:marc_schuetz
CentOS	Manual download		
Arch Linux	Community	Community AUR (git	Community AUR (git

		HEAD)	HEAD)
Gentoo	see https://wiki.gentoo.org/wiki/Dlang		
FreeBSD	Manual download Ports		Ports

Experimental compilers and forks

- SDC (Stupid D Compiler) - from-scratch D compiler implementation, written in idiomatic D.
- LDC for iOS - LDC-based toolkit for cross-compiling to iOS
- D for Android - Toolkit for cross-compiling to Android (x86 using DMD and ARM using LDC)
- Calypso - LDC fork which provides direct Clang interoperability, allowing the use of C headers directly.

- DCompute (LDC CUDA and SPIRV) - Library and LDC fork to "target CUDA and SPIR to enable hassle free native execution on the gpu" -upstreamed into LDC
- MicroD - DMD fork which outputs C source code instead of object files
- dtojs - DMD fork which outputs JavaScript source code instead of object files
- DIL - D compiler written in D2/Tango (inactive project)
- dscripten - LDC/emscripten-based toolchain for compiling D to asm.js / WebAssembly